T0196162

Eclectic
Poetry

A poem for every mood

Ben Sheldon

iUniverse, Inc.
Bloomington

Eclectic Poetry
A poem for every mood

Copyright © 2013 Ben Sheldon

iUniverse books may be ordered through booksellers or by contacting:

iUniverse
1663 Liberty Drive
Bloomington, IN 47403
www.iuniverse.com
1-800-Authors (1-800-288-4677)

ISBN: 978-1-4759-6212-3 (sc)
ISBN: 978-1-4759-6213-0 (hc)
ISBN: 978-1-4759-6214-7 (e)

Library of Congress Control Number: 2012921560

Printed in the United States of America

iUniverse rev. date: 2/1/2013

Contents

Section II: Relationships

Section III: Father Time

Section IV: Dark Side

Section V: Humor

Section VI: Play On Words

Section VII: Rhymed Poems

Section VIII: Haiku/Senryu

Section IX: Limericks

Eclectic
Poetry

SECTION I:
Thoughts

The Day Poetry Was Invented

Earth was once totally flooded
With jumbled numbers and mumbled words,
After incessant rains from thick clouds,
Of bureaucrats, self-centered professors,
And boring repetitious talkers.
To save the world from insanity,
A poet called No Ah built a boat,
With carefully crafted wood-strong lines,
From bobbing words that floated above
That ocean of forgettable babble.
That very day poetry was created.

Zilch

Much originates just from zilch,
And to nothing it all returns.
Sky gazers say all that they see,
Is countered by anti-matter.
It's out there pitch dark and unseen.
When the two types meet it'll be back
To silent nothingness for more eons.

These folks then tell us that's just how
It all started in the first place.
Matter and anti-matter split off,
In exact amounts in utter space,
During that super gigantic bang—
Only to disappear one day,
In a huge unfathomable poof!

And when we die we're sure to turn
From dust to dust to anti-dust then zilch.

Ads

Ad disclaimers are thrice
As fast as the main ad.
There should be a law
Requiring all main ads
Spoken as fast as
The disclaimers.

Journey

We start life in a baby's cage,
And end it in a wooden box.
In between them our paths zigzag,
Every which way all over the place.

Some tracks go over mountains,
Of achievement with road signs,
Like CEO or President,
With skeletons of former ones,
Strewn about the very high ground.

There are muddy paths some follow,
To other end of the rainbow.
They never reach it, all because
They're mired to the butts in their muck.

In time we all fall into ruts,
Rolling downhill to our boxes.

False Premise

I stood there as you dismantled
My proud persona fib by fib,
Prevarication from plain truth,
Leaving me with my naked fact.

Was numbed betwixt her cold details,
And the blustery North Pole winds.
Make-shift fig leaf of lie just failed—
Got sucked into her vacuum cleaner.

Fidelity

But I hear it in Low Fidelity,
Out of my expensive boom box.

Rain

Vast not impersonal ocean,
Feels warm loving stare of moving
Bright round eye, little people call sun.

Body of water gets the message.
It nudges eager jumpy molecules,
Into ever ready air mail

Carriers as cloudy emissaries,
To thirsty folks on parched city lands,
And rain good news in long flashes,
To thunderous heavenly applause.

Troubled Mind

Mind splattered with all them sorrows,
Will never wash very clean,
By psychic washer woman,
Nor by hypnotic head shrink.
At psychiatric laundromat,
Gallons galore of wordy bleach,
Tell you to see black deeds as white.
But it slides off like paint on rust.
Can't dry-clean heartbreak with worry.
One good way to remove dark spots,
From a good salvageable brain,
Is to wet-cleanse with some tears.

Artist's Way

To live I must breathe in oxygen,
Then exhale poetic words I can live by.
It's the way of surviving artists.
Without it we're vagrants of the world,
Waiting for Eternal Night to set in,
And wash away our existence,
Like ocean's tide over a lover's
Proclamation writ in sand.

Death Row

I write to you from Death Row.
You're reading this from the cell
Next to me; for we're all under
Capital sentence on Earth,
Biding our time on God's Death Row.

If one of us kills another,
And tips Heaven's hand early,
We play little gods and condemn him,
Into our little death row,
While we languish in the Big One.

Just Add Water

She left him for this rich playboy,
Living on Waikiki Beach.
Made for himself her favorite drink;
Added water to powder pile,
Giving him a Hawaiian punch.
All the time he felt like that shapeless
Little hillock of dried powder.
Wouldn't it be nice if unhappy
People came in such packets,
With instructions: "Just add love".

Anarchy

I talked to the Anarchist;
He warned me about Monarchy.
Chatting with a Monarchist,
She said: no king means Anarchy—
Ask a Frenchman or Iraqi!

Home

She cleaned about the attic,
Demolishing the cobwebs.
From a crack the spider watched,
With that inscrutable face.
Next day came a tornado,
To crumple the woman's house.
She eyeballed pile of rubble,
Just as the spider before,
Had stared at his fibrous heap.

Opportunity Knocks

I respond to every door knock.
Always people wanting this 'n that;
'Vote for my candidate and party',
Or 'be a Jehovah's witness'.
The banging is loud and clear.
In no time I'm off my rear,
Listening and chatting about
Highfalutin' stuff I'll flout.
When golden opportunity knocks,
It's so faint I can hardly hear it.
After TV and snacks I look;
Opportunity has gone!

Review

Reviewed my life the other day;
Unwound myself, rewound my thoughts,
And relived again—fast forward,
Like silent Charlie Chaplin movie,
Pushing a cart uphill past rail tracks,
While the train steams along closer.
Charlie, playing me, nears top then slips,
And rolls down over the rail road,
Just missing the chugging engine.
I've repeated that pointless effort,
So many times in my life across
Risky paths that looked deceptively safe.

Different Drummer

Nightclub doorman with eyes glazed,
And distant, as though listening,
To distinctly different drummer,
Snapped to now, snatching cover charge.

Inside, a few words escaped,
Through a thick blanket of noise,
Leaving chatters yearning for,
Some other place and partner.

The loud band played out of tune,
Tapping feet way out of step,
Like each player was hearing
A different drummer.

Placebo

Most people lead a placebo life.
From my comfy couch I've cheered Lance.
Drugged with a heavy doze of living, he mocked
His cancer, took Paris, won Tour De France.

Couch potatoes down their fake drug,
From beer cans to cure chronic doldrums.
They watch sportsmen go out play and compete,
For authentic elixir of happiness.

Tree

I learn a lot from a tree.
Through storm, wind and rain it stands
Its ground, though shaken and ruffled,
Fighting for its looser limbs.

Will cover winter nakedness,
With a flimsy cold cloth of snow,
Staying decent to well clothed eyes,
Till spring brings her grand green suit.

Novel

I took random lines of thought,
And threaded them together,
Into fabric of a story,
That's totally fabricated.
Dropped the ball of yarn-telling,
In path of cat-o-nine tails,
To whip up my fiction tale.
Can't crochet that into romance.
I continued to string up notions,
Of different colors together,
Into a brilliant novel.
All I got was a patchwork of quilt.

Neighbor's Cat

I gave them a ride to the vet.
The rash made pussy uncomfy.
Meanwhile the radio was saying,
Four thousand New Yorkers weren't comfy,
Either, in the World Trade rubble,

Beyond doctor's reach—in fact dead.
Life is full of contradictions.
World splits asunder under some folks,
With ungodly fire and brimstone;
Others worry to death about a pet.

Godzilla

Hugest most powerful giant,
On planet Earth, walks thump thump.
Nations shake and shiver at her growl,
Showing atomic teeth, spitting missiles.

She'll halt and shed a tear for victims,
Of hunger, disease, death and pillage;
And breathe out fire at oppressors.
It's a kind Godzilla, this USA.

Black Hole

Disturbing thoughts in orbit,
Inside my head turn and turn,
Like a hot sun around nothing,
Heading for gobbler black hole.

Then silent darkness of nothing.
With no black hole in my head,
To pull in 'n blast those thoughts,
They forever orbit my mind.

Dark

The sun got chopped like a tomato,
Going slowly down at sunset,
As neons and bulbs took over
The world in a tenuous fashion.

I looked up, surveying the sky;
The stars were lined up in rows,
Like pearly teeth in celestial smile,
As though saying: here comes the sun!

Double

Double your money in Vegas;
Then double it again.
If you keep it up you'll be rich,
Like Bill Gates and Larry Ellison.
Then you give to charities,
And people will forget you were
A professional gambler.

March

They march in columns,
One behind the other;
Each carries a bundle,
Twice its weight and follows
The wise leader ahead:
One, two, three, four, five, six:
Three legs left, three legs right,
They march and march—these ants!

Purchased Poem

I could not find all the right words,
To tell you how I feel for you,
So I bought a poem from this man—
A lonely wretched street peddler.

He'd found the secret verses I searched
In vain to showcase your birthday with.
Friendless, loveless, he still could love,
With these beautiful gifted lines.

Here they are, I read them to you;
I feel every loving thought,
Verb, noun and nuance in it—
But not a word of it is mine!

Amoeba

Has zero IQ,
Nor any eye Q.
No nose to smell
A good poem,
And knows it.
When near beauty,
It rolls away,
Without comment.
My good friend,
No-brain amoeba.

Russian Roulette

When inner feelings are hung,
On the wall for the public to see,
There is no sign that states:
"Delicate and soft, don't touch."
Most art connoisseurs enjoy,
And mull quietly and move on.
Every now and then I see one,
Artless who won't or can't read.
He pops up from nowhere special
To poke and maul at your soft innards
Of feelings, then shuffle off,
Leaving bruises and gaping holes,
As this live roulette bullet
Moves on to the next scared player.

Venge and Revenge

Eye for an eye makes the world blind,
Said India's Mahatma Gandhi.
If struck on left cheek turn the right,
Jesus told his Christian followers.
God told believers 'vengeance is mine'.
Martin Luther defied peacefully.

But a vengeful world rolls along.
Life for a life turns into tens,
Or hundreds in the Middle East,
Thousands in the New York island.

Then there is that deadly hatred,
Of a black man dragged by a truck,
Or gay guy crucified in the Middle West.
How did those nonviolent teachings,
Get bypassed into all this carnage?

Experience

Was told that insanity,
Was repeating same futile thing,
But expecting different result.
A wise bystander whispered: that guy
Will not learn from experience;

He can't see that same brick wall
He keeps smashing into.
This smart watcher also told me,
A true student of experience,
Can spot a glass barrier ahead.

High Society

Caviar, escargot, truffles,
Give me hives, make me real sick.
I sink deep till breathing stops,
Inside cushions of the Rolls Royce.
I'm allergic to High Society!
Smell of fish 'n chips draws me,
Like there's a magnet in my nose.
My bumpy Jeep is cozy,
Driving to Southern fried chicken.
Give me unpretentious folksy life!

Where Poets Crowd

All these poets gathered way down hill,
Even though poems got better going uphill.
Commenting on a posting way up here,
Someone dragged me downwards telling me
To quit wasting my time up there:
"Top poetry schmoetry! All action is at bottom!".
Descending Quality Hill I'd pause at gems,
But untimely tugs would soon roll me down.
When I reached the lowest level,
I was chest deep in verse-killing wordy weeds.
Below each patch of drowned poetry,
Was the poet's book for comments.
I picked up the lowest book to write on;
It was covered with mud as each page too.
Quickly putting it down I ran up the slope,
Along the lonely lines of better art,
Till safely out of the range of slung mud.

Why Do I Write

It don't pay and costs precious time,
To drain my brain and spill on screen,
For raves or rocks at self esteem;
Like going to war without boot camp.
So why do I keep on writing.
I'm caged in that skull of mine.
Strong sentences bend jailer's cell bars,
To dash for freedom—that's why I write.

Time Share

A large family, ours was.
Mother seemed always pregnant.
We each did our nine months and left
The womb, on a time-share plan.

Lived, we all, in a big house—
Home first to our granddad.
He passed it on to Father,
Then us, like a time-share plan.

Local Zoo

My boss is a little shrimp,
Who turns into a weasel,
Just when I ask for a raise,
Leaving work for early lunch—
A dozen buffalo wings.
I did not even know,
Those big buffalos had wings.

I saw one eat like a horse,
Then lumber out like a cow.
Some breed as though rabbit.
Others out-laugh the hyena.

In the market, bulls and bears,
Hug their white-elephant stocks,
As they wallow in dog's life.

Others are busy as bees,
Hobnobbing at flea markets,
Or giving gals the eagle eye.

All at our neighborhood zoo.

Homogenized

Added homogenized milk,
To my Starbucks coffee,
As they added ten more,
Of their cafes to this world,

Next to Kentucky Fried Chicken,
And Macdonald's hamburgers.
Issue isn't the finger lickin',
Or cheap food to kill the hunger;

They've homogenized my world

Rope

They tied Salem's witches with rope,
Without a whimper from the Pope,
As they prayed with no divine hope.

Infallible is the Holy See,
Came the word from across the sea:
It's God's law, don't you, laymen, see?!

At end of his rope was this priest,
After a night of sinful feast.
Found hanging, the priest was deceased.

Balloons

The kid blew the small rubber,
Into Mickey Mouse balloon;
Just like the kid had blown up,
From a small flimsy fetus.

A farmer pumped up a seed,
Into a forty pound pumpkin.
Pop goes the watermelon,
The flower and cauliflower,

From tiny planted specs,
Blown up with fluids of life.
We're a planet of balloons,
Eating off other balloons.

Intensive

Man in Intensive Care Unit,
Offered to buy one more day,
For a million dollars in cash.

What's worth doing for one day,
He was asked. "The usual," replied
The impatient patient with tubes.

Somehow he pulled through and went home.
Each million-dollar day was spent
Smoking and drinking on a couch,
Eyes on TV, mind in ICU.

Addict

She is beautiful, debonair,
Full of life and absorbing talk.
I took of her in small doses at first.

She gradually grew on me,
And I soon got hooked on her,
Like sniffing cocaine, enslaving ya,

With her air of free abandon.
I was addicted to her, when she split,
Leaving me alone in my detox home.

Gong

Stuck with the communist Gong Show,
From that Red Book of Moa Tse Tung,
Many Chinese fled like gangbusters,
Away from trials of the Gang of Five,
To the still-erect, not quite fallen gang
Of Falun Gong.

Law

The leaves fall down in Autumn,
Thanks to Newton's law of gravity,
As I gravitate to you,
Falling in love, just like the law says.

On a clear night we go to the moon,
At light speed, like Einstein decreed.
Airwaves stroke my eardrums, and I hear
Your gentle loving caress my ears.

We'd be lost without the laws of physics!

Dirt

Say what you will about dirt,
But it's my bed when I'm loveless,
And my home when I'm homeless,
Pulling over the sky for a blanket.

Leaks

Words swell in my head like bubbles,
In a boiling hot water heater.
A stream might leak in sentences,
Through silent moving lips that draw stares,

When accompanied by gestures.
It is never serious enough,
To summon men in white overalls.
Whirling mind can build pressures,

That blow open the safety valve,
And channel the leaking words,
Onto a pen that moves on paper,
Tracing a poem to tell a tall tale.

Schedule

Remember the tight schedules,
Of early life at school and college;
All in a tizzy with exams,
And quizzes that made us dizzy.

Then we were ready for real life.
Go to work then return home;
Lie on the couch and watch TV;
With no schedule, no progress.

Degree

Oh, the degrees of separation,
On my way to college degree.
So profusely I was rejected,
For days I sat and stared dejected,
Till this no-name school accepted
My detached concocted credentials.
Even they had some type of rules.
When caught cheating I got the boot,

Train Tracks

Between railway tracks I stand,
In abandoned pretty country.
Poets, artists who were here to admire,
Rode that train to escape
Predators that stalk beauty,
To smash, maul and abandon.

Here 'n there a bird will chirp
A poem or haiku to the wind,
In this just one-dog town,
Where the dog will pick a lovely tree,
To relieve himself of liquids.

SECTION II:
Relationships

Mud Wrestling

Disputes with a mud wrestler
Is very tricky business,
When it is all-important
To maintain a reputation
That's always been squeaky clean.

I walk around their mud pool,
Waving a plaintiff finger,
While they wallow in their slop,
Of filthy words and insults.

Sooner or later I get,
Their virus of rude conduct,
As they drag me straight into
Their cesspool of fuss and cuss.

Sharp

There are lots o' shops to sharpen knives.
I've heard words that cut much deeper,
Than all of them flimsy little blades.

Most puzzling in our sound babbling world,
Are ample supply of fine-honed words,
Not for cutting edge technologies,

But to cut each other up in talk.
So where do all of these people go,
To sharpen their words to the n-th degree?

They come back to slash at every turn,
In their cocky confrontations.

End

You said you want to end it all:
No one alive's worth living for!
Look at the Monarch butterfly,
Flitting from daisy to flower;

Isn't that worth another day?
How about that crimson sunset,
You have a date with every fall.
Never broken that one before.

For others you've always lived.
If not for yourself, how about
Staying on a little longer for me.

Mind Ceramics

I have a potter's mind.
The boss gives me a passing glance—
Neutral as a lump of clay.
I mount it on the wheel of my mind,
And spin away into fearsome monster,
That repeats: you're fired, you're fired!

Mom hands me a clump of loving
Complaint about mess left behind.
It goes right onto the whirling wheel,
Of her potter son who shapes it,

Into a lovely vase to hold
Handy dandy poison darts.
Even a compliment I can
'Twist 'n cover onto veiled insult.

Mind ceramics can be creative!

Book of Life

My life is an open and shut book.
A page is a day in my checkered life.
Blank sheet means I only breathed;
Thick volume is a brisk page turner.

Two thirds of it is completely blank.
Prologue of nine months by the publisher, Mom,
Is the far more readable section.
She talks to doctors and experts,

Sees psychics, gossips with neighbors,
And plots a life plan for the baby.
That would fill every sheet of a thick tome.
I see two volumes, nearing my tomb.

"Where did I go wrong?" I asked her old photo.

Flotsam

As river flows with flotsam and rafts,
So does the freeway with jetsam in cars,
Floating away from where not wanted,
Downstream to eddy into the backwater
Of an old friend whose sluice gate is open.

Discarded, they swirl back into water,
And drift onto the freeway's entrance,
Going with the flow to that elusive
Haven of love at the far end of the rainbow.

Rough

One can sleep on a hard floor,
To wake up with pains—
Tough on a settee of rocks.

It's like driving a bumpy
Steamroller with no shock absorbers,
On unpaved road full of potholes.

I can somehow find my way
Through the vagaries of life,
But without love it is rough.

Remote control

With my TV remote controller,
I'm king of every galaxy,
That's given a channel number,
And squeezed into that box with square
Aperture known to us as screen.

If a show takes me down more than
My usual tolerance level,
Of knee deep in crass raunchiness,
I close down the production
With a click, or turn them all mute.

Remote was in my pocket
One normal day at the office.
Secretary screeched on the phone.
Pointing the control at her mouth,
I pressed 'mute'; she stayed as loud.

At my job review, the boss was crude.
With remote at his face I clicked hard.
His channel wouldn't budge, 'cuz he rattled on.
Oh what I'd give for a remote
Controller that works in real life!

Split

You came in wearing a bib,
Sharp knife gripped tight in hand,
To say you love me no more,
And proceeded to cut up my heart,

And throw it at my whining pet,
Like some cheap brand of dog food.
Then you walked out in bloodied bib,
Leaving me heartless for next time
You show up at my door.

Little World

Every little world is built
To stand on shaky shoulders
Of two lovers who go steady—
Eyes level, and hand in hand.

They feel their delicate load,
And work carefully in sync.
If not, the whole world will tilt,
And slide into the home sink.

Parts

They gave him a lobotomy,
With good chunk of the brain gone.
Soon he had artificial legs,
Followed by a liver transplant.
Heart and lung replacement followed.
On mom's visit he hugged with his arms—
The only original parts left.
She hugged back like she had given birth,
To all those alien and man-made parts.

Together

I recall when our eyes first met;
The two minds joined into one.
We danced as our hands dovetailed,
United in matrimony,
Matched without a matchmaker.

In bad years wedges sprouted,
Between us watered by anger,
Like weed separating two roses.
It too withered, reuniting us.

When we dance the last tango,
Cheek to cheek, our wrinkles will mesh.

Watching from Outside

Once hot as a fireplace, our love
Is spent like old smoldering cinders,
To end up as a pile of ashes,
Soon to be scraped up and dumped,
Into that old dumpster of time.
I watched their house from outside;
Smoke curled out of the chimney,
And dissipated like our love.

Loss

I have written off this life,
With you, as a total loss.

If I happen to meet you,
Afresh in another life,
For heaven's sake do not start,
By blasting every bridge,
That spans a chasm to my heart.

Here and There

Glum faces sprouting out of
Humdrum clothing with drab colors,
Remind me of garden weeds.

I sprinkle my stuff on them:
A few quips here, a joke there,
And watch the face bloom to a smile.

I also use such weed killers,
As asking about their health,
How their folks are doing now;

They open up like a flower,
Emitting fresh new fragrance,
In touching human stories.

Borrowed Shoulder

For a long time I've been wanting,
To cry over your shoulder.
But yours was reserved for others.
So I wept on borrowed shoulders.

Haunted

I think of happy days of yore,
Forgetting you're dwelling in my head,
To knock off and perish the thought.

Something else squeezes into my mind,
To be brushed off and whited out,
With your handy Liquid Paper,

Quickly typed over: "me, me, me!"
No law can evict you from the innards,
Of my skull, you enchanting head haunter!

Memories

That moonlit stroll along the lake,
With its shimmering mild waves,
Is forever preserved in my mind,
As though with some mental MSG,

Short for Memory Saver Guard.
Picture of you in that carefree air,
Is permanently laminated,
And buried deep inside my psyche.

Caring smile amidst fluttering hair,
Stays fresh in my brain—deep freeze section.
I'll thaw and feast on it again,
When you are away and I'm real lonely.

Saving

It's so tempting to bandy
Love about on pretty faces.
Much like a shop-aholic
Run amok in Harrods or Saks,

And indulge as Willy Wonka,
Amidst chocolate-covered lust.
But I hold back and save my love,
For you, who's all heart with a big heart.

SECTION III:
Father Time

Eulogy

In time they'll eulogize me.
One who gave me early hell,
Will say how wonderful I was,
That he'll miss that face, now safely
Serene in velvet of the box.
In life, he hardly saw my face,
Talking from free-time cellphones,
Into them answering machines.

The boss will praise my great efforts;
How the company would suffer,
With me gone, omitting one thing:
He didn't give me a raise for years.

Eulogize me when I'm alive!

Train of Life

One-way train full of folks chugs along.
I was a day old when it pulled out
Of my birth place so long ago.
Wrinkles in the mirror tell me,
I have been travelling for years.

There are no scheduled stops on the way.
It will unexpectedly pause,
So a newborn baby will get on,
Gingerly placed in mother's lap,
To start its very own journey,
Through strange unseen landscapes.

Mom is suddenly sick enough,
To end her trip as the caboose halts,
Long enough for mourners to wave goodbye.
Surviving passengers resume their trek,
Until the train of life stops for me,

So I leave for my final resting place,
At a destination not of my choice.

One Lifetime

Myriad super plans I must do,
Before I take leave of this world.
Car that runs on water is one;
Begun research—boiling H2O.

Then founding a colony on Mars,
Is great after making clean cars,
With bags of money meant for the poor.
To make up we'll now house the homeless.

Dozen other projects I've drawn up.
Each one takes a lifetime to complete.
All I have is just one lifetime.

One Way Tracks

Mom put me on it from day one.
My train never stops, just chugs along,
At steady speed, though I think it
Is real slow growing up as a child,

Seeing no terminal in sight.
Seems to speed during love affairs,
And those unforgettable times.
Then down to a crawl at exam time,

Or endless funerals along the way.
Windows keep reflecting my age,
Zooming past retirement years.
I pull on the emergency brakes,

But my train of life keeps chugging,
Chugging, chugging just as fast,
To the terminal now in sight.
There, an oak coffin is surrounded,
By a crowd in black reading my will.

Black Wall

Huge dark partition looms ahead;
Gets closer as I grow older.
Masses of humanity,
Jostling just this side of that barrier,

Porous to ghosts that leave their hosts—
Bodies of the dying infirm.
Passage is always one way—
From our noisy part of the border,

To the deathly silence across.
No one I know ever came back,
To give us news of our loved ones,
Behind that sky high Black Wall.

Old Marilyn

She would have swished past eighty,
   If she'd lived to this day.

Can you imagine her dress,
   Heavy frumpy polyester,
Billowing up on the subway vent,
   Under Marilyn's callused feet.

Those quivering red lips, cracked and wrinkled,
   Next to her poster of long ago,
Is the bane of insomniacs,
   Just thinking of Grandma Monroe.

For the sake of lovely memories,
   And my sanity, you left in time,
Marilyn, and thanks Norma,
   For Monroe's worldly cameo role.

SECTION IV:
Dark Side

Them

Clad in a new suit, I passed them by,
On my way to a housewarming.
Them homeless in tattered clothes,
Stared at me as my gait faltered.

Suddenly I felt less elegant.
At dinner I scanned the menu,
Seeing them hungry eyes gazing,
Through the gourmet pages at me,

Burning off 'bon' from 'appetit'.
I see them whenever I'm pleased
With myself—in time to ruin it.
Someone plants them at strategic spots,
Where secret guilt feelings congregate.

Enron Affair

With stocks in hand I ran,
Value dropping with Enron.
Sought Arthur but didn't understand;
He also worked for Andersen.
I asked if it was really fair,
To retire on nothing but air.

Rwanda

Massacres of Rwanda,
Were too much even for one
Kind killer who called for civil
Maiming of victims, like chopping
Off of fingers and toes then wait,
To haul them to Chief for the count,
In finger semis and toe trucks.

From the ROTC Officer

In art class, I touched up a cute gal,
Instead of painting; got thrown out of class,
Adding a notch to separation;
Un-famous school expelled infamous me.
Air Force jettisoned my application.
Some call it cheat's poetic justice;
I call it degrees of separation,
While seeking a degree in desperation.

Smoke

Smoke gets in your eyes,
Soon after your lungs,
Curling out of your nose,
As you suck each Camel,
After killer Camel,
Till your horse face goes blue.
Meanwhile the actuary,
Knocks off fifteen years,
Off your life span.

SECTION V:
Humor

Judgment Dream

Woke up to Judgment Day, dreaming.
Screechy noisy giant trumpets played.
Graveyards all over sprang to life.
Those in blue gowns danced in circles;

Ones in yellow just watched perplexed,
While the red-attired were plain depressed.
Three lines, red, yellow and blue lead,
From here to the far horizons,

Each in a different direction.
Felt sorry for the red lawyer;
I gave him my blue gown and wore his.
He followed the blue line to Pearly Gates.

Saint Peter pored over the IBM,
(It's Been Missin') computer,
But could not find any lawyers.
He tried plea bargain with Saint Pete,

Who just threw a red gown at him,
And told the lawyer to go to Hell,
At the very end of that red line,
Where we met again at Hell's Gate.

Devil let him in then returned;
Scanned huge data base for my name;
Scratched his head in puzzlement.
He just could not find any poets!

15 Minutes of Fame

Everyone gets their fifteen—
Andy Warhol told me that.
His quarter hour stretched years.
Others bounce around that fountain
Of fame forever, like Bob Hope.

But I'm talking about mine—
My quarter hour of fame.
I can change any flat tire
Faster than anyone I know.
Not only that, my scrabble,
Is superior to Charlie's,
My neighbor, the bowling champion.
I'm good at other things too,
Like crossword puzzles and chess,
Not to mention filling bags
Of groceries dazzlingly quick.
Haven't had a driving citation,
Since I dinged aunt Martha's car.

So I didn't win a Nobel prize.
It's just my fifteen minutes
Of fame I'm still pursuing,
Like Andy Warhol promised me.

Saint Andreas

They live and prosper to a fault,
Along California's rickety line;
From business movers and shakers,
To Mormons, healers and Quakers.

Now and then there's a strong temblor;
Off banquet table slides a tumbler.
Corporate chief quits moving, starts shaking.
In church the Quakers turn tremblers.

They'll wait for God's second shoe to drop,
Then resume things with no blame game,
Knowing it was San Andrea's Fault.

Like Owner, Like Pet

Kitty and paroled owner moved,
To our neighborhood.
Soon murdered birds appeared in yards.
Feathered friends circled the cat box,

As the ex-con began to shoot,
In "cheap cheap" sound directions.
All we heard was: "cheap shot, cheap shot",
Over and over again—till cops

Took him away to the Big House.
His cat met a similar fate,
The owl told me; was tried
At Animal Farm, presided

Over by the Judge's bulldog.
Feline was convicted of nine counts,
Or birdicide and sentenced,
To nine consecutive life terms,
In the Dog House.

Got Mail

I punched into my e-mail,
Playing them keyboard keys,
Like a Liberace.
"All-male orgy" popped out;
Nimble fingers pressed 'delete';
Hitting 'next' brought in "Nymphs",
Which I fingered into e-trash.
Then flashed out 'cheap loans',
For my next million dollar home.
If I can't afford a nymph,
No way I'll buy a mansion!

Careful Christmas

'Twas time for Santa to take off,
From North Pole Heavenly Airport.
His sleigh was ready at the tarmac.
All eyes were on Rudolph's red nose,
To turn green as soon as cleared for flight.

Now Santa arrived at the terminal,
Belly shaking with "ho ho ho!" at kids,
Munching on Hihos and laughing "he he";
Then followed a mile long line of bags,
Wrapped packages of every size and shape,

That began to roll under the metal
Detector, with the cop caught off-guard:
"There's no jumbo plane to take all that!"
He moaned to the jolly old fella.
"I take them by sleigh—there's Rudolph, see!"
Beamed the red-coated heavy passenger,
Pointing at his shiny-snout pilot.

Quickly Santa stooped to pull up
The guard's jaw that fell to the floor.
"By Saint Nicholas that's impossible!"
Begged the worn-out airport watch dog.

"Noah put a myriad creatures in one arc",
Crowed Saint Nick; "this is a piece of fruitcake!"
By magic the lengthy line cleared up quickly;
Rudolph's nose shone green and Santa took off.

Check

They gave me hush money—
Unholy check that's signed,
By the Holy Father.
I put it in my bank.
The check bounced, stamped on it,
Across: "Return to Maker".

International Incident

Damaged Chinese spy plane landed,
At San Francisco airport with,
No permission, screaming May Day,
After a US plane got chewed,
By its propeller, plunging in sea.

America demanded that,
China apologizes for dead
Yankee pilot before getting
All their twenty four crewmen back.
Angry Beijing declared that they had
Nothing to be repentant about;
They were in international waters,
Doing legitimate surveillance,
Off northern California coast,
In full conformity with "our
Motherland's sacred obligations
To defend Chinatown from Yankee
Imperialists" they protested.

Needed

What the world needs,

Is redistribution,
Of retribution.
To avoid confusion,
With every infusion.

But the raver,
Will waver,
From Mao Tse Tung
To mousey tongue.

Cartoon

Sometimes I'd like to be a cartoon
Character without any worries.
If some mountain boulder falls on me,
It's true I get flattened like paper,
But in no time I pop back to full size.

No fuss, no mess left on the clean ground,
As I stroll home and greet relatives,
Congregating to hear my will read.
Seen a shocked person smile back at you?!

Bankrupt one shoots, bullet deflects off
My thick glasses, boomerangs to him.
Non-cartoon, he drops dead to my delight,
Just as kindly Porky Pig would've done.
Caviar for Easter? Plenty shows up,
Paid from ever so handy wallets.

Caveat: stay away from Bugs Bunny!

Rhythm

There is so much rhythm around.
Rhythm and Blues is staple
Of our numerous family,
Which had grown so very large,
'Cuz Mom's rhythm method failed.

Block

Chip of the old block,
Got mixed up with blockheads.
In a mental block,
He ran through a road block,
To tell his tale but had writer's block,
Missing on a blockbuster.

Escort

Called up escort service.
They required from me,
That I be handsome,
And fashionably dressed.
I failed in one,
And just passed the other.
Ain't tellin' ya which one
I flunked badly in!

Priorities

When big things head our way,
Priorities jump ship,
And our ducks in a row,
Take off every which way.

The band played bubbly music,
As the Titanic sank,
While some staff straightened out
The sliding furniture.

Widower at wife's burial,
Was asked if their football
Team won the sudden death,
Playing in overtime.

At wedding of plump wife,
Someone wanted to know,
From the pristine chaste bride,
When the baby was due.

An asteroid will one day streak
To blow us up on Earth.
Meanwhile some neat freak must dust,
To keep the house shipshape.

Wobbly Seat

Musical chairs we were playing.
All went around in circles;
Music stopped, I found a chair.
Next tune, it started again;
Everyone hovered around,
Each touching a near chair,
Before letting go to the next one;
The tune cut short as I grabbed
That pretty yellow chair I eyed,
Falling over, its wobbly legs
Slide off—landing on my butt!

Slippery Slope

I went for a little skiing,
On slopes of the tall mountain.
A slip felled me, rolling down,
Into a snowball that grew bigger,
Starting a roaring avalanche,
Towards our village down below.
Suddenly I stopped rotating;
Then there was a light at end
Of the tunnel dug by my brother.
I crawled out of a huge snowball—
That halted just short of our house.

How did he know I was inside?
My ski stuck out of the giant white ball!

Blimey

Wondering in London Town,
I'm seeking rich tourists,
Who could use a jolly good guide.
Bowler-hatted fella is looking
For his dropped monocle.
I stoop around and find it.
He walks off with nary a tip.
I give chase then pull on his sleeve.
Holding onto the bowler,
He says: "go away, peasant!"
Now that ain't very pleasant.
I poke out my tongue and blurt:
"Blimey, another Limey!"

Failed

What's her face, my English teacher,
Fails me in whatchamacallit test.
I wrote good with my thingamajig,
About all kinds of widgets,
And out-of-this-world gizmos.
She makes a do-da about
Every dohickey I do,
As when she stepped on my dog's doo-doo,
Like I was some old fuddy-duddy.

Diagnosis

A checkup showed it was stomach ulcers.
The second opinion was from a plumber,
Who was dabbling in psychiatry.
He kept hammering into my head,
That my problem was psychosomatic.
His diagnosis hit the nail on the head,
Even though he couldn't spell 'psychosomatic'.

Symphony

Was told of unique symphony,
Just arrived to play in town.
My taste is not hifalutin',
So I demurred despite rave reviews.
But they play Beethoven divine;
Mozart music shall surely shine.
"Don't belong there" I stood my ground.
"They play their music in the nude",
Whispered the mousey one in my ear.
"I just love Mozart and Beethoven",
I blurted out to all: "let's go!"

Memory Not So Sharp

She raved about the great movie:
"Tree Grout", starring Wayne Newton.
It turned out to be "True Grit",
With the super star John Wayne.

She talks about circular service,
After attending a secular meeting.
At the restaurant she wants 'peeking bird'
Having had, before, Peking Duck.

I get confused going out with her.

Melissa

She's now an octogenarian, she said.
No more 'peeking duck' or other meat for her.
Even at thirty 'twas preposterous, I said.
Prosperous or not, anyone can do it,
She shot back, sipping from a V-8 can.
Good word for a V-8 vegetarian,
I conceded, as she scorned my English,
Blaming it on my junk professor.
It's adjunct, I sheepishly corrected.
Ancient History she's into nowadays.
Winking confidently, she asked if I knew,
The Romans loved animals and worshiped zoos?
"No", my shy reply; "wasn't their god Zeus"?
I whispered, hoping not to lose her.
She frowned and closed the door behind.

Wild West

The Wild West has not changed much.
It was cowboys and Lone Ranger;
Now it's salesmen and Loan Arranger.
There were gun battles at Dodge City;
Today with drug battles we dodge the city.
O.K. Corral shootout wasn't alright;
Tougher now to corral marijuana kids.

Wok

In China chefs come from all woks of life;
From wok on fire in a prime club,
To the vending street woker.
They always slowly wok not run.
Orders show on a round woky talky,
With Chin Yee woker Whiskey.

Bugsy

Bugsy came back as Bugs Bunny,
To check on Las Vegas he started,
And find the Mafioso who killed him.
But the mobster had died and returned,
As that fast talking Porky Pig,
Whose hobby was hunting for wabbits.
They conclusively proved that the hell
Of the afterlife need not be hot!

Deposition

The lawyer was full of it,
Giving trial deposition.
After feeding his fat face,
For two hours in lunch buffet,
He rushed to the bathroom,
For another deposition.
Seated, he figured his hefty fees.
Out, face flush, he's set for court.

Allergy

Like different foods, people are.
There's that cute one I could eat,
With any kind of dressing;
Better still with no dressing.

Then the type I'm allergic to.
Smothered in the best dressing,
And garnished with grand jewelry—
They still make me very sick.

Jungle Roundtable

In far-out animal kingdom,
Galloping to camel lot,
Was brave, dashing Sir Ocelot,
With sidekick rhino, Sir Gollyhead.
Camel lead them through the desert,
Onto the sea to pick up Marlin,
The great magician of King Kong,
Who royally suffered from arthritis.

12 Men

Twelve angry men in Cape Town,
Judge and test him for poor judgment.
Still he thinks himself lucky.
Deep inside the thick jungle,
His brother is eyed and tasted,
By twelve hungry men—cannibals!

Language

This language still confuses me.
Just bought a refurbished computer;
Was it furbished in the first place?
What do you do when you furbish?

Boulevard

I was born on Sunrise Boulevard,
Oh, in some little East Coast town,
But wish to die on Sunset Boulevard,
Where it's chic to bid final farewell.

Oral

He failed every written test,
Despite direct line to God.
Verbal stuff he always passed.
He is Oral Roberts.

Good Art, Bad Art

Good art draws connoisseurs,
Like buzzing bees to honey.
Bad lines pull looky-loos,
Like flies onto cow dung.

Quite often the dung guys,
Are smart as the honey gals.
It can be romantic,
Lost in their semantics.

Worth

Overheard a voice saying:
"If I can buy you for what
You are really truly worth,
Then sell you for what you think,
And believe you are worth,
I'll make a fortune!"

Bear

Bear with me as I explain,
How a word leaves one barely sane.
NRA wants to bear arms.
Car sticker flaunts: "The Right to Arm Bears."

Some wish to shear bears for wool,
Or for fur, or barely so.
If it catches on, think bare bears.
I'll stop here, while barely a bore!

Abortion

Poor mom didn't abort her baby.
In slums he grew up with bad boys.
His gang cut short a good man's life.
With her kid on Death Row,
Mom couldn't halt this abortion.

Ann Believable

Despite her teenage youth,
She'd always tell the truth.
The girl was so credible,
It is incredible.
Her tales were so believable,
It is unbelievable!

High Art

High art you must forego,
If you suffer Vertigo,
And have nowhere to go.

Fathom

Some things I can't fathom.
Did algae come from Algeria?
Or albinos from Albania?

Cousin

Went to see old kissin' cousin;
Was shocked to hear a cussin' cousin!

Salt

He adds salt to sea water;
Is shocked it tastes the same.

Emperor's Clothes

Fashion gurus say: clothes make the man;
Case in point: the emperor's new clothes,
With the latest see-through French fabrics.

Wind

The wind blew continuously;
She would not stop talking.

Rush

You rush less when you're there;
So why is it called Mount Rushmore?

Freedom

Give me liverty,
And some whiskey.

Bars

Barman behind the bar,
Served drinks to teen gals.
He now serves behind bars.

Mr. Thritis

I know a man called Art Thritis.
He spends his time in all the joints.

Pin

I heard the pin drop,
Made a hellish racket.
Huge pin weighed two tons!

SECTION VI:
Play On Words

Shackled

Capped cop held a hubcap.
Chuckled at shackled man with shekels.

Nagging Doubt

In the nightmare of a dream,
there galloped a knight on mare.
Heady horseman held nagging doubt,
about his hesitant doubting nag.

Sinner

I met a seaman
Who did sin bad.
They called him
Sindbad the Sailor.

Uncouth

The man was very uncouth,
But always tried to be couth,
Since he was a small youth.

He's older now and long in tooth,
But still mean; and that's the truth.

Push

I'm pushing thirty five
And often getting pushy.

Dad is pushing seventy—
By no means a pushover.

Granddad's no longer with us;
He's pushin' up daisies.

My cousin may soon follow
The fate of all drug pushers.

I can halt time, dye my hair,
Whenever push comes to shove.

Caveats

At Pearl Harbor it was 'Tora! Tora'.
Then came Afghan caves of Tora Bora.
Armed kids bomb, then read Bible or Torah.
They come from New York to Walla Walla;
Some as far away as Bora Bora.

Section VII:
Rhymed Poems

Pick a Pickle

Big and tall, that's Chuck,
With tiny brother called Chuckle.
He gave shorty a buck,
So when in the car he'd buckle.
Years ago was bribed to suck
Milk bottle, to wean him off suckle.
Little ones can't choose 'n pick.
Blamed, they're always in a pickle.

Odd Things

I saw some odd things in my travels,
Seeking new topics for my novels.
There was a fat yak in a kayak,
With whom the paddler would yacketyyak.

At Disney World the bark of a tree,
Kicked a barking dog who'd come to pee,
While a cat played with a can o' peas,
That rolled off a canvas canopy.

In Arabia, a grand ruling sheikh
Slurped, by Allah, milkshake— so un-chic—
Purchased with two-for-one coupon,
After his Rolls was stopped for Grey Poupon.

Carnival at Rio and Amazon
Spotlighted Brazil nuts; 'twas amazin'.
Robed men from Tonga danced the conga.
Decked gals of Congo swung in tango.

Voo Doo

When you do voo doo,
You won't blurt one boo boo.
Just satanic poo poo,
Sidestepping mind's doo doo.

Teacher

I was taught Creation,
By a teacher who's Croatian.

His wife was some pest,
They'd met in Budapest.

Flight

Put in your fare at Travelocity.com,
They'll tell you the bargain trip to fit your money.
I typed in "twenty million dollars" to see the outcome.
The screen went haywire with image so loony,

Then clear message: "Return moon trip in Russian rocket."
Closer to Earth, I checked for mere ten thousand bucks;
Found I'd fly the Globe five times in small seat bucket,
With airline quite adept at avoiding airborne ducks.

Darn, I can only spare fifty greenbacks this year!
What the hell, I typed the figure in and waited:
'Twas a glider flight with an outfit of no peer.
Waving a finger at the screen, I screamed: "Forget it!"

Evidence

He was struck by a leg of lamb,
Frozen piece of meat hit on the head.
Killer skipped town gone on the lam,
With a victim in the freezer—dead.

Thus began a tale so chilling;
Wife cooked the leg, served with elegance,
To fat detective checking the killing.
He sat there eating the evidence.

Secret

I know the secret of Las Vegas.
Got address of every winking lass.
For a fee I'll tell ya ones with sass,
And the gazelle from catfish and bass,
If you're not just after a piece of ass.

SECTION VIII:
Haiku/Senryu

1

The elephants walk,
In straight line, trunk to tail.
A hyena laughs.

2

Full moon, through cloud gap,
Spotlights lovers on park bench.
Shy spinster walks fast.

3

Dove with olive branch,
Flies into very thick smoke.
Tired firemen seek peace.

4
Sluts and slot machines,
Intermingle with pawn shops.
Glitter of Reno.

5

Beth's baby was cute.
Named Mac 'cuz had no known dad;
Henceforth called Mac Beth.

6

Inside, poet writes,
About beauty of nature.
Outside, red sun sets.

7

Lion cubs playing,
In the rain on fertile land.
Rainbow's far away.

SECTION IX:
Limericks

Gaelic

There was a loose, hot poet who spoke Gaelic.
On her legs were writ lines sexy and slick.
She stood atop Stonehenge.
Druids went on reading binge.
Even blind men used Braille to get their kick.

Hawaii

There was a young man from Hawaii;
He drew fishy gals on Waikiki.
Once, he caught a mermaid.
Couldn't be eaten or laid,
He beached her to hook mahimahi.